Author: Martin Fritzen, Second edition, 2019©

Graphic designer: www.kornerupdesign.dk

Publisher: Books on Demand – København, Danmark

Production: Books on Demand – Norderstedt, Tyskland
                     This book is produced by an on-Demand-proces

Photo credits: pexels.com

ISBN: 978-87-4301-327-3

GRASSROOTS ESPORTS

How to Build A Successful Grassroots Esports Organization

Introduction

This book is designed to give you the blueprint on how to build an esport organization and provide you with an inspirational catalogue of ideas for you to securely manage the operation and development of your esports team, organization or esports club. Plus, you will be armed with amazing science and arguments, as to how and why, esports benefit the society as well.

Esports are booming - commercial events, packed arenas, amazing prizes and great shows are becoming the norm! Awesome teams, players, managers, sports psychologists, streamers, casters... and so much more!

People, young and old, male and female - almost everyone - is into computer games, in one way or another.

In Denmark, esports activities are being offered alongside sports like football (soccer), volleyball and swimming in sports clubs. As of January 2020, there are more than 200 traditional sports clubs across Denmark, with more than 7,000 paying members (players), offering esports activities to the community and their local area.

Grassroots esports groups are growing and it is amazing! We see new players, coaches, managers and sponsors all wanting to be part of the esports scene!

Why this book?

Starting, organizing and building an esports team or organization is hard and expensive. This book is written for esports teams, organizations and sports clubs working with esports. My mission is to provide a wide range of ideas and ammunition so you can develop and run strong, structured, profitable esports teams and organizations.

In 2015, I founded what is now one of the biggest esports organizations in Scandinavia with several teams and coaches, as well as hundreds of paying members and profitable revenue streams. In 2017, I was hired as the Esports Project Manager at Danish Gymnastics and Sports Associations (Danske Gymnastik- & Idrætsforeninger) (DGI). DGI is a sports association in Denmark that works to better the conditions for more than 6,500 member sports clubs and their more than 1.5 million members. My job is to lead a team of 14 people to develop esports activities in the 6,500 sports clubs around Denmark.

This book is a collection of successful experiences and strategies from over 200 esports clubs and organizations around the world. This book is designed to give you the blueprints on how to build an esport organization and provide you with an inspirational catalogue of ideas to securely manage the operation and development of your esports team, organization or sports club.

The suggestions found in this guide are all based on my personal experiences working to help build grassroots esports around the world. All the advice that I give you has been tried and tested for esports organizations of all sizes, and I hope that it will help yours as well.

Key takeaways in this guide:
1. Develop strong teams and work with great people.
2. Build a unique mission statement based on your core values and vision.
3. Set simple and clear goals.
4. Plan 1, 2, and 3 years ahead.
5. Reduce your costs.
6. Understand why your organization is unique and how you can make a difference to partners
7. Secure the revenue streams you will need to achieve your goals.
8. Understand how you make profit and how you scale your business.
9. Work hard and focus on partnership sales every day.
10. Be quality-oriented in everything you do.
11. Continuous development and learning.

Happy Reading,
Martin Fritzen

About the author

Martin knows all about success in esports. He founded what is now one of the biggest esports organizations in Scandinavia with several teams and coaches, as well as hundreds of paying members and profitable revenue streams. He is now leading esports activities at DGI - a sports association in Denmark that works to better the conditions for more than 6,500 member sports clubs and their more than 1.5 million members.

For the last few years, he has heard the same question over and over, "How can we make money to develop and run our esports team or organization?" This book is based on years of experience building and creating sustainable esports organizations with relevant partnerships, as well as several years of talking with esports organizations and companies sponsoring esports.

"I hope this book will inspire you to think outside the box so you can begin to build profitable revenue streams and achieve your esports dreams, just like so many others." – Martin Fritzen, 2020.

12

How to start, structure and organize an esports organization

In Denmark, we have three ways of doing esports. I'll walk you through each one – it might be of inspiration to you and others.

1. ESPORTS, THE COMMERCIAL WAY

This kind of esports is the "easy" kind; venture capitalists (VCs), businesses, brands and/or individual founders and business owners, join competencies, experience and capital, and create an esports organization. It typically contains at least one esports team, sometimes more.

They form a new business and build a strong brand. They pay for the top players, coaches, trainers and managers. With some of the best players, they can win big tournaments, and prize pools, thus building a better brand while also gaining media coverage of the team –resulting in selling team merchandise. This is seen in Denmark with Astralis Group, who works with their brands Astralis, Origen and Future FC. As of December 2019, Astralis Group became the first esports team to launch an initial public offering (IPO). Astralis Group went public on the Nasdaq First Growth Market Denmark, offering 16,759,777 shares at 8.95 Danish Krone ($1.33) apiece, according to ESPN's Jacob Wolf.

Astralis Group may be a pioneer, but launching an IPO can potentially set the precedent for other organizations willing to take the plunge. With esports quickly becoming one of the biggest industries in the world, investing in the scene may seem like a no-brainer. Global esports revenue is expected to hit $1.1 billion this year, marking a 26 percent year-on-year growth, according to a report by research group Newzoo. The 2019 League of Legends World Championship finals peaked at 2.9 million viewers, almost doubling last year's totals. And Comcast Spectacor and The Cordish Companies put together a $50 million plan to build the "largest new-construction, purpose-build esports arena in the Western Hemisphere" within the Philadelphia Sports Complex. The industry is growing rapidly and Astralis Group's decision to open up shares to the public further cements esports as a titan to rival film, music, and sports.

Even though esports is certainly trending upward, some may be reluctant to invest in the relatively new field. "In this respect it is also our responsibility to help educate the market through a continuous high level of information," Astralis Group chief executive officer Nikolaj Nyholm told Bloomberg. The Danish organization's Counter Strike: Global Offensive team, Astralis, is the top-ranked squad in the world, according to HLTV. Astralis Group also owns League European Championship (LEC) team Origen and FIFA's Future FC. Credits: Andreas Stavropoulos and dotesports.com.

Pros: With many financial resources, you have the advantage to be able to pay for great talent, coaches and trainers, and thus, providing great training and travel experiences.

Cons: One disadvantage to the commercial method is that it takes a lot (a lot) of money and can be hard to build/manufacture a team bond and spirit. It can be difficult to create the cult fan base culture, around the "cold and capitalistic" brand (but possible).

2. ESPORTS, THE EDUCATIONAL WAY

Throughout the world we are seeing more and more educational institutions; primary and secondary schools, as well as higher educational institutions + universities, offering esports classes, courses, teams, clubs and organizations. This puts esports directly in the educational curriculum, sports programs and recreational activities.

Different schools offer different esports courses, some of which have 200+ students and major classrooms and arenas, with state-of-the-art-gaming setups specific for esports.

Others offer advanced esports courses in gaming tactics, teamwork, communication, healthy diets (for gamers), exercises and so on. Some schools have smaller setups with fewer students, who bring their own laptops, and play together. In these cases, there is not as much technical esports teaching, but rather the courses help develop social skills and provides a fun atmosphere. Which is another good option that is also beneficial to a different group of gamers – more social gaming, than competitive esports.

My point is, educational institutions are embracing esports in many different ways and experimenting to understand which setup will fit the individual school and its student's needs.

Pros: To bring esports into the educational system is great, and it will grant both the gamers, and esports (as a sport), the recognition and strong reputation that is needed, to develop even further. This is extremely important in order to attract sponsors, VCs and create amazing esports tournaments and events – and to develop great talents.

Cons: There can be really big differences in the teaching-skills and experience level across teachers, instructors and coaches. It can also be difficult to create curriculums, as well as finding funds and a budget for esports facilities. Which is why, every country must have a national esports federation to develop and offer centralized esports coaches, instructors and teachers-courses and educations.

3. ESPORTS, THE SPORTS CLUB WAY

Right now, esports are tapping into traditional sports clubs across the world.

More and more of the traditional local sports clubs and associations are experimenting with starting up esports departments alongside their existing sports – and that makes sense!

I am from Denmark, and Denmark might be unique but I wanted to share a bit more on how Denmark is doing esports, the sports club way– perhaps it will help you in your city/country.

Volunteers
Without volunteers, there would be no sports in Denmark.
The structure of the national federations and grassroots sports clubs in Denmark is democratic. A general meeting is held every year and a president, board members, treasurer, etc. are elected or re-elected every second year. A group of volunteers run the club who appreciate and share openness and joint responsibility. Some of the elite clubs and teams have paid staff but the primary tasks in the local clubs are taken care of by volunteers.

Sports leaders, coaches and helpers manage the daily duties such as mowing the grass on the football field, putting out the ropes in the swimming pool and gathering members of the club for training or social activities – the same goes for the clubs offering esports. We see volunteer team leaders, game tacticians, streamers, casters, coaches, event crews and managers all work hard voluntarily. But why?

Sports, and esports, attract the kind of people who want to share their love of the sport with new people and generations. They can be sponsors, players, trainers, staff, and other volunteers but in the end they are involved so that kids across Denmark are able to enjoy esports training, boot camps and tournaments alike. Through the sport and community, kids will also develop as people and gamers.

This will help the gamers earn the respect and recognition for their personal development and gaming skills.

Funding
In Denmark a law called, "The Act on Youth and Adult Education" ensures municipal financial aid for leisure time and educational activities such as local sports. It is executed in the form of grants to sports activities and rent for indoor and outdoor facilities. Apart from the financial help from the municipalities the local clubs are funded through annual or bi-annual membership fees, which are usually quite low.

Sponsors are also commonly used as a source of additional resources/funds.

For everyone
It is very easy to become member of one of the thousands of sports clubs in Denmark. Most clubs offer an introduction period for newcomers to get an idea of how the particular club works so members can become accustomed to the environment (before getting charged a membership fee).

All clubs gladly welcome new members into their "family" at all times of the year. Whether it is to participate and play the sport or just to help out as a volunteer, all people are accepted on equal terms. A simple phone call to the president of the chosen club will provide more information, while you could also reach out to the national federation, who is able to assist finding a local club near you.

Esports benefit from this mentality too. This means that you can visit your local club, have a chat and join their esports division. If the local club does not yet offer esports, you can do one of two things,
1) offer to start up the new esports division at your local sports club, or
2) find another sports club in the area that already offers esports activities.

Pros: Participating in esports in the traditional sports clubs is smart because you start with a standing structure, an organization, a treasurer, a board, and a location – in essence you'll have a "home" and a brand name – and maybe even a budget.

Cons: There can be huge differences in competencies, experience and commitment among the volunteer coaches, trainers, leaders and managers within the esports club's administration and management. Also finding funds, while possible, is always hard.

4. ESPORTS, THE COMMUNITY WAY

So you must think I can't count, but actually, there's a fourth way to esports – bootstrapping, the old-school-way of doing esports. This is more gaming-related and takes place when gamers in clans, guilds, or other gaming and esports communities (typically online – through a game client) join forces, create teams, and start entering tournaments and competitions together and/or with friends. You can easily create an esports team with your friends and start going to online or onsite tournaments and develop from there.

The community teams can easily talk to their local sports club, and start-up a new esports division, if they do not have one already. They can also start up a completely new sports club. This is all because of the "The Act on Youth and Adult Education" law in Denmark that provides the support and gives the community teams the possibility to find rooms or a building, and attract economical grants and funds. These benefits are only given to registered official Danish sports clubs – so you can see the benefit for a "community" team to join with a sports club.

Pros: The community way is an easy and free way to start up a team and join esports tournaments.

Cons: It can be difficult to maintain the team and build structured training. Also, it can be difficult to attract funds and sponsors because you are, essentially, on your own and not a part of a club or brand. Unfortunately, many community esports teams and organizations have started and closed down after only 6 months, because the funding was too thin or the people were too inexperienced to lead and manage a team.

My personal favorite way of esports
I love that esports are becoming more and more a part of sports clubs and the educational system. Why? Because my heart beats passionately for "little Michael" or "little Sarah" (all children growing up) who love to play games on their computer, phone or tablet. I, especially, feel for those who have not been given the proper respect, or recognition for their personal growth and/or gaming talent.

Fun fact: Defense Command Denmark is testing gamers to see how well they can perform in the air traffic controller education: an education only obtainable for 5% of the population, because it is so difficult.

"When we test applicants for education, we focus on spatial intelligence, strategic sense, fast responsiveness and the ability to keep a calm overview even under extreme pressure - and it is, among other things, essential for playing demanding computer games," says psychologist Jimmi Andreasen, who works in the selection department of the Ministry of Defense's Personnel Board (FPS).

I am rooting for all the people, organizations and businesses working towards spreading esports in a way that builds confidence, a feeling of self-worth, a sense of meaning in life and friendships among our society.

The worldwide esports scene is thriving and growing as I write this and I am grateful to play a part in it. Esports in schools and sports clubs will build a great talent pool and form a solid organizational structure around esports; while commercial esports will secure top performers from professional teams and players.

9 Steps to start an esports organization, association or club

Now I want to share my personal experiences from building a grassroots esports club. Let´s go!

This guide is based on my experiences from founding and being chairman of the board at an esport association in Denmark. The esports association is one of the biggest esports club in Scandinavia, with 300+ paying members and 100+ volunteer trainers and managers, as of January 2020.

WHY START AN ESPORTS CLUB OR ASSOCIATION?

I love sports clubs! I grew up close to my local football club. You could even say I lived there most days of the week playing football, making friends, having fun and improving my football skills. I never wanted to become the world's best football player -- that was for someone else. I just loved my friends, the practices, games, trips, boot camps, fights, wins and, maybe not as much, but our losses too. Oh, and it did not hurt that I met my first girlfriend through my football team.

Sports clubs create a space for people to grow, to develop self-worth, to find a sense of meaning in life, to create friendships and relationships and – yeah – love.

This is why esports fit perfectly into existing sports clubs and why it makes sense to start up an esports club. An esports club creates the framework for friendships to grow and allows people to gain recognition, respect and confidence. People develop personal and social skills, while learning and improving their esports talent.

I believe in human potential
When people ask me, "Why did you start the esport association and work with esports on a daily basis?" My answer is this, "Esports create recognition and respect. It develops people and helps to trigger talent and potential. This is why I work with esports: I believe in releasing human potential".

STEP 1: START WITH THE "WHY?"

The first thing you should do is ask yourself the following question, "Why do I want to start an esports club?"

Next, go somewhere where you can find inspiration and think of ideas (Note, you do not have to find the "right" answer, just brainstorm so you get an idea of what you will build – and how to do it). Ask yourself again, "Why start an esports association?" and consider the following:

What are your goals?

What are the values you will work from?

What is your mission and vision for the club?

Who do you know who also knows about esports?

Do you want to form a locally based club, an online club or a hybrid?

Which location will the club members play at?

What equipment should the members play on?

What games will the members play?

How do you find trainers to coach members?

How do you find a board of directors for the esports association?

How do you find sponsors and economic and legal assistance?

How do you find competent people to work with?

Thorough preparation is half of the work! The biggest mistake I made when starting up an esports club was thinking I could do everything myself. Once I started to involve other people, who also loved esports, and each working in their field of expertise (sales, marketing, HR, law, administration, gaming and finance) things started to accelerate really fast.

I can also advise in finding board members, team leaders and managers who come from outside the esports and gaming communities. These people create great value by asking questions and suggesting ideas that gamers do not.

Great! Now you have a game plan.

STEP 2: GET IN TOUCH WITH PEOPLE

Here there are two ways to go:

1) You are already in a traditional sports club playing tennis, running or doing other cool activities. If so, you should set up a meeting with the club manager or board members and present your game plan. Ask if the sports club is interested in you starting up an esports division within the club.

This is a good way to build an esports club, because you start with an already existing platform, brand, name, colors and have access to a board, accountant, bank, sponsors and so on. Oh, and usually a new esports division provides great press, new members and new energy to a traditional sports club. Traditional sports clubs can also have difficulties attracting or maintaining teenage boys and esports can help.

2) If you are not associated with any club, I would suggest that you contact your local sports club, and present them with your game plan. You could also start up your own esports club, with no association to a club.

I believe that being associated with a local sports club, due to the benefits listed above, is the best option. If you want to start from scratch, contact your local government or municipality, set up a meeting and present them with your game plan. You want to learn how they can assist you in creating an esports club, which grants you can apply for, and if they can help you find locations, equipment, computers and so on. Most cities in the world, offer some assistance when citizens want to start up social, cultural and/or sport-initiatives. Now you know how to start an esports division with an existing sports club or on your own. You have met with both sports clubs and the local government, to understand how to do so. You know which legal permits you need and how to officially register the esports club, so you can apply for funding, grants and receive other social assistance from your city.

Fantastic! Now all the paperwork is done, let's move on.

STEP 3: FINDING ALLIANCES AND BOARD MEMBERS

When I started the esport association, I met with the chairman of the board and he asked me to bring my game plan and eight names for the esports board. The following week I came back with 14 pages of a detailed game plan and a list of ten people, who I wanted to be part of the esports club.

How? I created a Google form where interested people could sign up. I shared it on social media and asked if anyone wanted to start a local esports club with me (unpaid/volunteer work). They could sign up and I would contact them. Then I invited the candidates for a meeting. They were adults with different professional and gaming experience; I needed people who could do the things that I could not.

It is important to build a board with a variety of competencies. Look at a person's skills, rather than age or experience. In the end, our board consisted of four people with gaming experience, three people with no gaming experience and myself as the chairman. As a group we had professional experience from banking, education, sales and marketing. We were all unpaid volunteers but all members, coaches and board members paid a membership fee to be part of the esports club.

Once you have recruited the right people for the board, you can sit down and show them your game plan again. I suggest discussing your plan on an operational level and figuring out the answers to these questions first:

What should you call the club? What will your logo, colors, website, social media, streaming profile and so on, be?

Which games should you offer training in?

How, where and of what frequency should your members train?

How do you find coaches? (and educate them?)

What does it cost to be a member?

How does money come into the esports association?

How can you work together with parents and schools?

How many members do you want?

Are your members going to tournaments? If so, how?

Should you hold your own events, if so, how? - And many other topics.

Your goal will be to create the foundation and framework for the esports club. If you are part of a traditional sports club, there might be internal rules on colors, shirts, and brand names that you should be aware of.

Now you have made the first framework for the club. Great Job! Let's move on!

STEP 4: SETTING GOALS

Right, with the board in place, and your newly formed framework, you are ready to start working on setting goals and operationalizing your plan. See the framework and plan as dynamic and remember that in just six months (or even less) there may be a lot of changes and it may require you to re-do some parts.

Here are some suggestions for goals:

We will offer training in xx game, starting on xx date

We will associate xx number of coaches to xx game, starting on xx date

We will be xx number of members, by xx date

We want sponsorship income for xx amount by xx date

We want an active website, Facebook page, or Twitch by xx date

We will stream xx times a week, starting on xx date

We need xx players participating in xx tournaments, xx times this year

We will host xx number of our own events this year - and attend xx number of others' events.

Being specific like this force you and your board to become detail oriented. This ensures that fewer mistakes are made and maximizes your chance for success. Try using "Smart" as a mnemonic device to remember the kinds of goals you should set for yourself: S, specific; M, measurable; A, achievable; R, realistic; T, timely.

Way to go! Now you have specific goals to work with.

STEP 5: STRATEGIZE!

By this point your board has made a game plan and set relevant goals. Now you need to make a strategy for how to achieve these goals.

A strategy can contain the answers to these questions:

How do you select which games you want the group to be trained in?

How do you find coaches for the relevant games? (Be specific here)

How do you find partners, sponsors, finances, a location, equipment, etc.?

How do you create marketing material and tell stories about your activities?

How do you secure a steady increase in members?

How do you deal with legal requirements in player contracts, partnerships and events?

How and which events will you attend? (If this is a goal)

What is your strategy for amateurs and elite players in your club?

How do you establish partnerships with schools, municipalities, regions, parents and others?

This might sound similar to the other points, but the fun part is that when the board starts discussing strategy, you will find subjects that are discarded, and others that you will work more in depth with.

The biggest mistake I made was not working close enough with the members' parents and not working close enough with schools. Also a recurring question we asked ourselves was, "Do we want to pay (with money) members to play for our club?" Another strategic question is "Do you want to pay the members' tournament-fees?" This question came up frequently for us.

When you have figured out how you will work on these matters, you have the first strategy in place for your esports club! Amazing, great job!

You are ready to hand out tasks and start working!

STEP 6: WHO IS DOING WHAT AND WHEN?

Let's make an operational plan. Your board has created a strategy for achieving your goals based on your game plan, values, mission, vision and general ideas.

Now it is about putting it into action. The board should compile and prepare an operational plan for who is responsible for each task and by a certain deadline.

The operational plan has the answers to the following:

Who is responsible for creating sponsorship agreements and by what date?

Who is responsible for associating xx trainers to xx games, and by what date?

Who establishes cooperation/meetings with schools, municipalities, regions, etc. by what date?

Who is responsible for creating a website, Facebook page, marketing material, etc. by what date?

Who is responsible for establishing premises, equipment, uniforms, etc. by what date?

In short, allocate responsibility and deadlines for the goals you want to achieve.

Let me highlight that, no, you will not be able do everything on your list perfectly. Start with the things that are easiest for you and the board to do. Make mistakes, correct them, get better, listen to your board and your members and ask them what they want and how they feel, and work from there. Always improve and correct your mistakes along the way. Always be curious and interested in how you can make the club better.

However, hey, great job! Now you have an operational plan for your goals!

STEP 7: LET'S GOOOOO!

Now your board has prepared everything as thoroughly as possible. You have competent people; you have a plan, goals, and strategies and have divided responsibilities and deadlines.

So now it's about executing the plan. Esports clubs have many stakeholders and therefore you may find that many people want to meet and talk about what you are doing.

Most municipalities and regions are interested in supporting esports in some way. The same goes for most youth and higher education programs such as IT, DATA, and technology education. Media and local businesses are also interested in local sports/cultural activities.

STEP 8: STOP!

Evaluate and adjust.

As time goes by, you will find goals or plans need to be changed or completely replaced. Make sure you, on the board, talk about the success of what you do. For example, if it doesn't make sense to make a big esports tournament, well, don't do it. Do more of what works, and do less of what is difficult or unsuccessful.

My success at the esports association was partly because everyone working there was volunteering and, not to mention, worked very hard every week to create the best possible results. Most importantly, they wanted to provide the members with the best possible esports experience.

Amazing!

Now you have a working esports club with a functioning board, paying members, active coaches, valued partners, sponsors and interested schools and parents. You offer online/onsite local training in xx games, xx times a week. Maybe you offer esports tournaments open to local gamers? Maybe you offer bigger esports events, where people travel longer distances to participate? Maybe you offer your members online/onsite tournaments? Maybe you offer esports boot camps, summer camps or summer school, where you teach subjects like esports communication, team building, diet and health, how to behave and act online, game tactics and other amazing stuff! Great job! Things are working out for you!

Sooo, what now?

STEP 9: KEEP GOING!

Next up - operations and development! The months following the start of your esports club will include evaluation, customization and execution of your plans. In my esports association, it was important to first find the right format for training and practicing. We discussed and implemented the following:

How to recruit the right coaches and managers (unpaid/volunteer)
Customized meeting agendas

New games, new coaches and the creation of local tournaments
Constant focus on establishing collaboration with partners that matched the strategy of the club

Strong focus on our finances and growth

To promote communities, friendships and human development
Ensure that our coaches, managers and board are happy, even though unpaid

Ensure that our members feel happy and heard

And a lot of other stuff, I can't remember ;)

Contact with the members, team leaders, coaches and trainers is extremely important. Ask them what they think and want. Ongoing evaluation and customization provides value and ensures that the association/club keeps momentum and optimizes time and resources on the relevant things.

I believe in working closely with media and journalists as well. You can get great media coverage in traditional media as well as more modern forms. Make sure you set up streams and find engaging casters to build an audience for your club. And make sure you have great social media reach, and build quality content, articles, newsletters, player profiles, team profiles, board profiles, and share game results. Invite the media to practices, tournaments, and boot/summer camps. This will give you massive coverage, increase your member base and attract sponsors.

A little about PEGI

PEGI (Pan European Game Information)

In Denmark we see the PEGI recommendations as that, recommendations, not law. This means that we have esports clubs, and schools, where they offer training in CS:GO for youngsters, below the PEGI recommended age. Why?

I believe that people learn best through trial and error. How can we learn to master things, if we don't actually try and fail? This allows kids and adults to build skills, competencies and learning about persistence. In our schools and sports clubs we can offer good educated trainers, managers, coaches, teachers and leaders who can educate our players. This way, our players learn even when below the PEGI recommended age, how to communicate; how to handle pressure inside and outside the game; how to be a good teammate; and how to behave respectfully towards the game, the team, managers, parents and other players. This positive behavior transfers outside the esports club and schools to homes, families, and friends.

By educating our players, we can help them develop great behavior both when gaming and in their private lives, which we have seen helps players gain new friends and become more social and positive in school.

Gambling, betting and esports

Gambling, skin betting, casinos, betting, money, wins, losses – are all words we see as a part of our esports world. In Denmark we (at DGI) work closely with The Danish Gambling Authority and the National Center for Gambling Addiction to ensure that we provide a large amount of information, education, training and courses to esports clubs, parents, managers, coaches, schools – and of course, the players themselves. Our intention is to create a strong and safe esports environment, for our players to excel within.

So, you might think that we, Danes, are liberal and free, in our approach towards PEGI and its recommendations. But, in fact, we have seen and learned, that we can do a heck of a lot more to help, guide and educate schools, esports clubs, players, parents and managers, by having them organized in schools and clubs, instead of having everyone sitting at home alone.

What about money and huge prize pools in grassroots esports?

Personally, I do not like money or huge prize pools in grassroots esports for the simple reason that I have seen how players can enjoy playing just for the fun of it—the friendships, the experiences and the pride of winning.

Don't get me wrong, I think it's fine to have prizes for the winners, best teams, best players, and all that. And prizes like cups or trophies are amazing. When it comes to esports with kids and teens below 18 or 21 years old, I think monetary prizes should be secondary.

I have seen it in practice myself. In October 2017, we filled the concert hall of Esbjerg (Denmark's 5th biggest city) with the finals of a grassroots esports tournament. We had teams traveling from all over to battle each other in CS:GO, on stage, with a fantastic setup, sounds, lights and an amazing caster. We had six teams in the finals and more than 1,000 fans on site-- and no monetary prizes.

These were all grassroots players. Some players have tried other tournaments, but for the most part, this was their first tournament. It was the first time that the majority of the players played on a stage. They got to sit next to their teammates on a stage, playing in the finals, and in front of all their fans. Many told me it was amazing and an experience they will remember for the rest of their lives.

While this example is, perhaps, small compared to the rest of the esports world, it shows some of the motivating factors in grassroots esports: friendships, experiences and memories for life. Grassroots esports players want to continuously develop their skills while at the same time they want to make friends and be a part of something bigger than themselves. They want to grow as people, and as players. They want to experience new things and be proactive in building grassroots esports. Some gamers get more involved by becoming tournament crew, or by becoming coaches, team leaders, casters, web designers or fundraisers.

I see grassroots esports players, coaches, and team leaders as people who want to make a difference for their club, for others, and for themselves. This is why I believe in grassroots esports. It provides a place for people and friendships to grow and in the end the individual player, coach, team leader and manager will feel like (and are) a meaningful part of something bigger.

Should we be afraid of computer games and grassroots esports?

The answer is simple, no. I believe in "everything in moderation". It's natural to fear new things, especially new technology. I have collected four anecdotes about new technology through the years and the skepticism around each one.

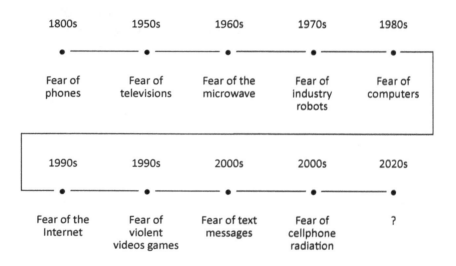

1800s	1950s	1960s	1970s	1980s
Fear of phones	Fear of televisions	Fear of the microwave	Fear of industry robots	Fear of computers

1990s	1990s	2000s	2000s	2020s
Fear of the Internet	Fear of violent videos games	Fear of text messages	Fear of cellphone radiation	?

The printed book
In the 1500s a German goldsmith named John Gutenberg invented a machine that changed the world: the printing press. The books and materials that were produced via the printing press did not come without resistance.

Already 400 years before the birth of Christ, the Greek philosopher Socrates (who never wrote a word himself), thought that the written word would lead to forgetfulness. In the 1600s a Swiss biologist, Conrad Gessner, said that books gave an overload of information and that the population should be spared.

200 years after the invention of the printing press, the philosopher Gottfried Wilhelm said that books were spreading and creating barbarism and cruelty. However, the printing press paved the way for the Enlightenment, Industrial Revolution, moon landing, Nokia 3310, Fifty Shades of Grey and much more.

The Radio
When Guglielmo Marconi invented the radio in the beginning of 1900s, he wrote a letter to the ministry of Post of Telegraphy, where he applied for financial support for his radio project. He never received an answer but instead he was awarded asylum for insanity. No one in the ministry saw the opportunity for a wireless music box.

When the radio was further developed from a 1:1 communication tool to a broadcasting device in the early 1900s, it caused a stir and many believed the wireless music box was worthless and that no one would pay to receive impersonal messages. When the radio gained popularity it was met with hard criticism. The radio was accused of being distracting for children doing their homework and thus hindering their education and the future of society.

The Phone
In the 1800s a revolutionary technology was invented. It consisted of copper wires and electromagnets and provoked great resistance and skepticism. In 1877, the New York Times wrote that the invention would destroy privacy and some critics among others, author Isaac Funk, believed that the invention was a risky move to erase the boundaries in the real and spiritual worlds.

Others believed that the invention would turn society into a collection of anonymous and isolated individuals. The invention was originally described as a remote device; today we just call it a phone.

The Internet
During the 1990s it became possible for the common person to use a telephone cable for more than a phone call. The magazine Computerworld, wrote in 1993 that the "Connection to the global Internet now has [a] low price where private consumers can join".

Many were excited, while others were extremely hesitant. For example, the Danish newspaper, Politiken, wrote in 1998 (journalist Henrik Palle) how the people feared that the Internet users would be transformed into soulless info-zombies with squared-eyes and faces that would neglect family and friends. Palle continued by saying that Internet users would only be able to survive if the local pizza place was online and delivery. The article also said that the Internet could lead to a world populated with "webaholics" and info junkies, where even tiny babies must send electronic letters to their parents for breastmilk and attention. Fortunately, it didn't turn out quite so bad.

With new inventions, new technology and new habits, comes fear, primarily a fear of change. We like life as it is and are not as ready for changes as we would like to be. Thankfully though, children, tweens, teens and first movers are. They embrace new technology, play with it, and make their own.

As a school, sports club, manager, coach, parent or responsible human, we can help youngsters by informing them, educating them and bringing esports/gaming to them as a club, association or course. We can take an active part in their education and be a part of the new "world".

42

Reaching those who are marginalized in society

I want to share a short story about a boy who his fictional but is based on real life experience.

Meet Ali, he is 10 years old, and lives in a big city in Denmark – in an area that most people would call a ghetto. Ali's parents are from Pakistan. Ali likes to compete. He is a fast runner and hard hitter. He steals bikes and sometimes candy from the store. He is not that interested in school, even though he is rather smart and he could do well if he wanted.

Ali has, what is called, a negative/destructive social network. His friends are older and they ask him for favors like "getting" chips and drinks for them. Ali does what they say because he appreciates the recognition and the feeling of meaning he gets when performing these tasks for the older boys. He becomes part of a group.
One day the local sports club hangs a poster on the wall saying, *"Red Star Sports Club, now offers esports and gaming activities – come check it out, and meet us".*

Ali has never been in a sports club. He likes the streets where he feels safe and comfortable. On the other hand, Ali loves computer games. He plays FIFA and Counter Strike, with his friends and he is talented. When he plays, he often wins, and people usually want to be on his team if possible. He decides, with a few friends, to join the sports club and check out the esports activities they offer.

A visit to the esports club
A big friendly man at the entrance of the sports club greets them. Smiling, shaking Ali's little hand, he says, *"WELCOME little man, just go inside".* Ali smiles, he already likes the huge man.

They all go inside and are guided to the esports room. Ali feels like he has been struck by lightning. He is amazed. The room is packed with people, talking, laughing, smiling and playing. The room has 20 gamer PC setups, 3 PlayStations and a huge television, streaming some of it. In the other end of the room there are a few couches and chairs for relaxing, hanging out or watching a movie.

There is a meeting room, a strategy room and suddenly the huge man comes back, claps his hands loudly and yells, **"EVERYBODY, LISTEN UP, HEY, LOOK AT ME"**. The room becomes silent and he starts to talk.

Ali is dazzled and a little distracted by all of the esport-equipment and people, so he doesn't catch everything the huge man says. He does hear, though, that the club offers FIFA practice for kids 9-12 years old, Mondays and Wednesdays. That's all Ali needed to know. As Ali and his friends walk home, happy and impressed by what they experienced, Ali says, *"I am definitely going to see what their FIFA practice is all about"*.

The following Monday rolls along and Ali is not so sure about going anymore. Should he leave the streets where he feels safe and at home? Yes, he decides, at least he should try it. He already plays FIFA every day, so what's the worst that can happen?

Ali laughs to himself as he walks to the club, dreaming about being the best in the club, beating everyone else. As Ali walks into the esports room he notices a few other boys who are there, and a young man, who immediately turns to Ali, gives him a big smile and says, *"Welcome to Red Star FIFA practice, I am Mo, who are you?"* Quietly and a bit shyly, Ali replies, *"Ali"*, Mo points towards the PlayStations, where five other boys are playing FIFA and says, *"Great, we are expecting a few others and we start at 5pm. Go have a game with the others while we wait a few more minutes"*.

I´m simply the best!
Ali walks slowly toward the other boys, when suddenly Mo yells, "Brian! Say hi to Ali!" A boy turns around, smiles, hands Ali a controller, and says, *"Hi, I am Brian, this is Mohammed, Sali, Matt and Mark – are you any good? We need a good team in order to compete in the FIFA tournaments and league this year"*.

Ali feels welcomed and they start to play. Quickly he scores one, two, three goals, and wins the match. Brian high-fives Ali and says, *"Well played Ali, nice!"* Ali figures out that Mo is the coach. As the clock hits 5 pm, a few more guys enter and Mo closes the door. He gathers the nine boys in the conference room and starts to inform them about FIFA practice, and the FIFA division in Red Star Sports Club.

Ali finds out that he needs to be a member of the sports club in order to be a member of the FIFA division. He has to practice every Monday and Wednesday and needs to stay out of trouble and take care of his schoolwork. The club works closely with the local schools, local government, social workers and police. And if the club finds out that any player is involved in any crime, drugs or is falling behind in school, they will take actions and possibly suspend the player from the club.

Ali gets it — this (sports club) is a kind of reward he has to earn. Being number one drives Ali. He wants to be the best.

The sports club offers practice hours, as well as the opportunity to participate in tournaments locally and in the national league. Ali discovers quickly that he is one of the best and Red Star is doing really well. They are even playing at bigger tournaments where they travel by a bus (that the sports club owns), and where Ali can play on a huge stage in front of – what looks like – hundreds of people.

His friends back home notice that Ali is at the club more and more, and less and less on the streets and with them. They ask him why he is playing FIFA. It makes no sense to them, why not join them and go back to stealing bikes and candy.

Ali doesn't hesitate when they confront him and says, *"I can't risk my place on the team and I want to play FIFA. I want to show everyone that I am the best!"*

Hard work pays off
Ali is struggling personally. His friends are challenging his commitment to the esports club, school is hard, and his mom and dad do not want to pay for a membership in a sports club. Mo, the FIFA coach in the club, sees that and has a chat with Ali.

Usually, Ali is not talking to anyone about his feelings, but with Mo it's different. He respects Mo for his honesty and straightforwardness. Ali has never experienced anything else from him but respect and recognition. So Ali feels safe talking to Mo. It's not like Mo has all the answers but he offers to talk to Ali's teacher, so Ali can get a little more help in school. Also, Mo praises Ali for choosing the sports club over crime. As they speak, Mo realizes that Ali has made a few good friends in the club as well. So they agree to figure out if Ali could see Brian or Mohammed outside of practice at the club. Lastly, Mo informs Ali that the local government offers a grant that he can apply for, which will provide Ali with a free membership to the club. Ali feels like everything is falling into place. Amazing.

As time goes by, Ali develops into one of the best FIFA players. He puts a lot of hours into the game and starts to jog for exercise, because it's important to have a fit body and mind when doing esports.

His family starts to come and watch him play tournaments. When his mother and father see him on stage, winning and receiving a huge cup they agree to pay the membership fee to the club. A couple of years pass and Ali finishes primary school with an acceptable result. Now he is a veteran of the club. One day, Mo comes to Ali and asks him if he would consider becoming a coach and train the new boys who have just started at the club. Without hesitation Ali says, *"Sure, when do we start?"*

The story about Ali is based on many young kids I have met in Denmark over the last 15 years. The name could as well have been Michael, Sarah or Yusufa. When sport clubs, schools, local governments and social workers work together, and form projects based around passion and interests (as esports are), we see certain hard-to-reach groups begin to interact and grow in a positive way.

Unfortunately, a lot of gamers and players are being bullied, called names and teased for the fact that they game or "play on the computer" – even from their own family and friends.

Esports, when well-structured and organized, provides gamers a community, recognition, a feeling of self-worth and a sense of meaning. This can be crucial for a person's personal development and in the end, a person's feelings about living a meaningful life

Self-Esteem & Esports

All over the world, we have boys and girls - men and women who love esports. All types of people love to play games on their computer, console, tablet or phone – some in groups and some alone. This fact, in its self, is a dilemma, because many of the people closest to the gamer, like friends and colleagues, do not get it – the love for the sports. Even most gamers' families do not understand why they chose to sit in front of a screen constantly instead of going outside and getting some fresh air.

We, as humans, seek and appreciate other people's recognition. When we are acknowledged for our work, hobbies, and/or athletic or academic ability – we feel social approval.

The positive attention from others makes us feel that we are accepted and that builds a person's self-esteem.

Let´s get the concepts right:
1. **Self-esteem:** To feel trust in one's abilities, qualities, and/or judgment
2. **Self-confidence:** To feel confident in one's own worth and/or abilities

You can have self-esteem, without feeling confident and you can feel confident, without having high self-esteem. The two are not mutually exclusive.

In return, when friends, family and colleagues disapprove of our passions, for example gaming, we feel bad and ashamed. In some of the worst cases people are bullied, mocked, and made fun of, which is not really a part of building strong, functional humans.

Let´s take a look at some theory here...
The Self-Determination Theory (SDT), developed by researchers
Edward L. Deci and Richard M. Ryan, concerns human motivation,
personality, and optimal functioning. Consider the phrase "optimal
functioning".

I like the idea of it and isn't that what we want for anyone—*to
function optimally?*

The hypothesis of SDT says that people have three basic psychological
needs: competence, relatedness, and autonomy. When these needs
are fulfilled, people are empowered to function optimally and can be
successful in their lives.

Competence
The need for competence means that humans have the desire to
control and master the environment and outcome of their surroundings.
We want to know how things will turn out and what the results are of
our actions are.

An esports example: When we are working and playing around/in
esports games, we feel competent.

Relatedness
The need for relatedness in the SDT deals with the desire to "interact
with, be connected to, and experience caring for other people".
Our work and daily activities involve other people and through this,
we seek and fulfill the feeling of belonging.

An esports example: When we play games with others, work with
others, or simply just talk to people about our game(s), we feel
connected and relatable. The stronger the connection is, the better.

Autonomy
The need for autonomy concerns the urge to be causal agents and to
act in harmony with our integrated self. Deci and Ryan believe that to

be autonomous does not mean to be independent. It means having a sense of free will when doing something or acting out of our own interests and values.

An esports example: It is important to actually allow players to be players and let them play, work or study the field they are passionate about – esports.

Motivation

This leads me to consider motivational theories; what is it that really motivates us? Deci researched giving positive feedback based on performance on an activity and whether or not this increased intrinsic motivation. Deci came to the conclusion that positive feedback *can* satisfy people's need for competence and this can, in turn, enhance our intrinsic motivation. Positive feedback is seen as a social approval.

Receiving positive feedback can increase self-motivation due to our need for feeling competent and wanting to belong and connect with other people. Moreover, affection and verbal approval are not seen as a controlled stimulus, and therefore intrinsic motivation tends to increase. Ryan & Deci (2000) define intrinsic motivation as, "doing of an activity for its inherent satisfactions rather than for some separable consequences".

Simply put, an individual is intrinsically motivated to do something when they like what they are doing. For instance, gamers love to game for the sake of the activity itself, for the positive experience of performing and not for the potential secondary gains that may arise from doing what they love.

WHY ESPORTS IN CLUBS ARE IMPORTANT

We now know that in order to feel motivated and function optimally, it is important to feel competent. It is important to have relatedness and to be autonomous. You can experience these three factors in harmony in esports when those who have the passion for the area, have jobs or educations within esports or gaming. This is the same for esports and gaming clubs and associations, where most activities are based on passion, gaming and volunteer work.

I believe that every single gamer should become a member of a club, whether it's at a school or at a sports club, I do not care. When gamers become members of something bigger, we, as a society, have the opportunity to create social learning and provide a place for friendships to grow, skills to improve, parents to be included, and most importantly, the players have people and places to go to, when in need.

I believe in clubs, communities and associations. I believe that governments should support clubs offering esports activities. I believe in clubs where friendships grow, where great coaches and role models can teach and educate players, and where gamers can develop as member of a group, rather than sitting home alone. I believe in building economical and ethical esports clubs where players can feel at home and where people can grow as individuals and as players because that is what I have seen works in real life.

Take Home Message
The Self-Determination Theory claims that people have three basic needs: competence, relatedness and autonomy. When these needs are fulfilled, people function optimally and feel empowered to achieve their goals and dreams in life. Gaming and esports are based on love and passion for games and competition. Gamers are intrinsically motivated and by playing in a club, with friends or on a team, they can get the three needs from the SDT fulfilled. I recommend that every sports club in the world offers esports activities and by that, play a part in building empowered, successful people.

Esports & Labor Skills

I have also analyzed some research and data on the effect of gaming on labor skills. I have always suspected a positive relationship between gaming skills and skills that could be applicable in other professional industries so I wanted to look more into it. I discovered that the research does suggest that video gaming can improve labor skills, however, the evidence on the effects on cognitive and motivational skills seems more compelling than the evidence of effects on emotional and social skills.

Google Scholar, PsycINFO, and Pubmed were the three databases that were used. I also focused on recent studies instead of older studies. According to Granic, Lobel, and Engels (2014)[1], labor skills include four domains: cognition (e.g. attention), motivation (e.g. resilience in the face of failure), emotional (e.g., mood management), and social (e.g. prosocial behavior).

Cognitive skills are particularly important in jobs requiring rapid decisions and a broad overview (such as air traffic controllers), whereas motivation in the face of challenge is an important competence in jobs involving problem-solving assignments (such as software development jobs). Emotional skills are important in care and nursing jobs and social skills are essential in all types of jobs involving human interaction.

1   Granic, I., Lobel, A., & Engels, R. (2014). The Benefits of Playing Video Games. Am Psychol, 69(1), 66-78. doi:10.1037/a0034857

In study *The malleability of spatial skills: a meta-analysis of training studies*, Uttal et al. (2013)[2] examined to what extent training programs improved spatial skills and whether gaming could produce equivalent spatial skills improvements. The authors meta-analyzed 217 research studies on spatial skills training and concluded that spatial skills can be trained. Furthermore, they concluded that commercial video shooting games produced the same improvement in spatial skills as 1) school programs targeted at improving spatial skills and 2) laboratory training with specific spatial skill exercises. Thus, shooting games can improve spatial skills to the same extent as targeted school subjects and laboratory training.

Chiappe et al. (2013)[3] examined whether action videogames can improve multi-tasking in high workload environments. 53 American university students (18-36 years) with no action videogame experience were pre-tested using the Multi-Attribute Task Battery (MATB), which measures multitasking skills. Following this pre-testing, half of the students engaged in playing action video games (Ghost Recon 2 and Unreal Tournament 3) for a minimum of 5 hours a week for 10 weeks. All students were then retested with the MATB. The results showed that the group of students who had played action video games were better at managing multiple tasks, and the authors concluded that action videogames can increase people's ability to take on additional tasks by increasing attentional capacity.

---

2   Uttal, D. H., Meadow, N. G., Tipton, E., Hand, L. L., Alden, A. R., Warren, C., & Newcombe, N. S. (2013). The malleability of spatial skills: a meta-analysis of training studies. Psychol Bull, 139(2), 352-402. doi:10.1037/a0028446

3   Chiappe, D., Conger, M., Liao, J., Caldwell, J. L., & Vu, K.-P. L. (2013). Improving multi-tasking ability through action videogames. Applied Ergonomics, 44(2), 278-284. doi:https://doi.org/10.1016/j.apergo.2012.08.002

Venture et al. (2013)[4] examined the correlation between gaming and persistence during difficult tasks among 102 American university students. The authors measured persistence by recording the time spent on unsolved anagrams and riddles in an online test. The participants also completed a questionnaire on how many hours a week they spent playing video games. Results showed a positive correlation between time spent on playing video games and persistence, which means that frequent video game players spent more time on unsolved problems relative to infrequent video game players. The authors concluded that gaming can improve persistence.

Adachi and Willoughby (2013)[5] examined whether strategic video game play (i.e., role playing and strategy games) predicted self-reported problem-solving skills among a sample of 1,492 Canadian adolescents. Participants were asked if they played strategic video games and if they played fast-paced video games (i.e., fighting, action, racing). Participants also completed a questionnaire with five items regarding problem-solving skills (i.e., "I think hard about what steps to take" and "I think about the choices before I do anything" and "I tell myself 'Stop and think before you do anything'"). The authors found that more strategic video-game-play predicted higher self-reported problem-solving skills over time than less strategic video game play such as fast-paced games. In addition, the results showed support for an indirect association between strategic video game play and academic grades.

---

4   Ventura, M., Shute, V., & Zhao, W. (2013). The relationship between video game use and a performance-based measure of persistence. Computers & Education, 60(1), 52-58. doi:https://doi.org/10.1016/j.compedu.2012.07.003
5   Adachi, P. J. C., & Willoughby, T. (2013). More than just fun and games: The longitudinal relationships between strategic video games, self-reported problem solving skills, and academic grades. Journal of Youth and Adolescence, 42(7), 1041-1052. doi:10.1007/s10964-013-9913-9

THE EFFECT OF GAMING ON EMOTIONAL FUNCTION

Gaetan et al. (2016)6 examined the relationship between video gaming and emotional functioning such as emotion regulation, emotion intensity, emotion expression, and alexithymia among 159 French adolescents. The participants were asked if they played video games regularly and from their answers, the sample was divided into "regular gamers" and "non-regular gamers". Furthermore, the participants completed a series of questionnaires on different dimensions of emotional functioning. Results showed that regular gamers were more active in regulating their emotions and felt their emotions more intensively. Results also showed that regular gamers engaged in less emotion expression and that they were less able to put emotions into words. The authors concluded that that video gaming is not unambiguously enhancing emotional function and that more research is needed.

THE EFFECT OF GAMING ON SOCIAL SKILLS

Durkin and Barber (2002) 7 examined the relationship between game play and several measures of adjustment and risk taking in a sample of 1,304 16-year-old American high school students. The participants completed a questionnaire asking if and how often they played video games. They also completed a series of questionnaires on wellbeing, adjustment and risk taking. Results showed no negative effects on gaming and showed positive (favorable) effects on family closeness, sports involvement and other social activities, engagement in school, mental health, drug use and peer relations. The authors concluded that gaming can affect the social development of adolescents positively.

---

6   Gaetan, S., Bréjard, V., & Bonnet, A. (2016). Video games in adolescence and emotional functioning: Emotion regulation, emotion intensity, emotion expression, and alexithymia. Computers in Human Behavior, 61(Supplement C), 344-349. doi:https://doi.org/10.1016/j.chb.2016.03.027

7   Durkin, K., & Barber, B. (2002). Not so doomed: computer game play and positive adolescent development. Journal of Applied Developmental Psychology, 23(4), 373-392. doi:https://doi.org/10.1016/S0193-3973(02)00124-7

Additionally, Gentile et al. (2009) [8] summarized three studies examining the relationship between prosocial games and prosocial behavior among Singaporean, Japanese and American children and adolescents. All three studies showed a relationship between prosocial games and prosocial behavior. Specifically, the studies showed that prosocial video games enhanced short-term helpful behavior and that children playing prosocial games at the beginning of the school year behave more social during the end of the school year. The authors conclude that the three studies provide robust evidence of a positive effect of prosocial games on prosocial behavior – short term and long term. In addition, it is proposed that violent video games can also enhance prosocial behavior if they center on corporation rather than individual competition.

A quick summary of the research
Regarding **cognition**, two studies were summarized of which one showed positive effects of shooting games on spatial skills and one showed positive effects of action videogames on multi-tasking skills.

As for **motivation**, one study showed that video gaming can improve persistence during difficult tasks and another study showed that strategic video game play predicted problem-solving skills.
Regarding **emotional function**, one study was summarized which found that video gaming is not unambiguously enhancing emotional function.

Finally, two studies on the effect on **social skills** were summarized. One study found that gaming can affect the social development of adolescents positively and another study found that prosocial games can enhance prosocial behavior.

---

8   Gentile, D. A., Anderson, C. A., Yukawa, S., Ihori, N., Saleem, M., Lim Kam, M., . . . Sakamoto, A. (2009). The Effects of Prosocial Video Games on Prosocial Behaviors: International Evidence From Correlational, Longitudinal, and Experimental Studies. Personality and Social Psychology Bulletin, 35(6), 752-763. doi:10.1177/0146167209333045

In sum, this brief report on research studies supports the notion that video gaming can improve labor skills in other industries outside of gaming. However, the evidence on the effects on cognitive and motivational skills seems more compelling than the evidence on effects on emotional and social skills.

A Case Study: DGI Esport in Denmark

DGI is a national umbrella organization for more than 6,000 local sports associations and clubs in Denmark. The sports clubs represent more than 1.5 million active members and a wide array of activities including for example gymnastics, badminton, basketball, handball, shooting, volleyball, swimming, tennis and various martial arts. With 15 regional offices across the country, DGI covers all of Denmark as well as a small part of northern Germany.

The main idea behind DGI is to encourage Danes to join their local sports clubs and associations and to ensure positive and motivating environments in which athletes can thrive and develop regardless of their skill level and physical capabilities.

Esports
Because of the explosive growth of esports in recent years, DGI decided to establish an esports department – DGI Esport – in 2017. DGI Esport supports the development of esports in Denmark and works to educate the public on the benefits and potential of esports. DGI Esport is founded on the belief that esports has the power to create a strong sense of community and to motivate new groups of people and kids to join a club or association. The goal is to create positive, motivational and stimulating esports environments with room for players of all kinds – regardless of age and skills.

Growth
DGI Esport promotes the development of esports, helps establish new esports clubs around the country and works to ensure that esports become an integrated part of associational life in Denmark. They offer customized concepts to help individual clubs attract new members, develop new activities and achieve their full growth potential.

With a team of esport experts, DGI Esport provides counseling and expertise on a wide range of issues including finances and funding, equipment and facilities, games and activities as well as ethical issues such as gambling and betting.

With IT solutions developed specifically for sports clubs combined with a wide range of administrative services, they make daily routines and tasks easier for the clubs. The administrative services include book keeping and marketing, and their services free up time and allow the esports clubs to focus on areas such as strategic development, which allows clubs to improve their concepts and attract new members.

Training and education for esports coaches
Together with esport experts, players and clubs, DGI develops training and education for esports coaches to improve the overall quality of esports training and activities, and to ensure a continuous focus on player and team development. DGI's belief is that skilled coaches and high quality training are key factors in attracting, engaging and retaining members and consequently, education of esports coaches is an important tool for creating growth and development in esports clubs internationally.

The training concepts at DGI include a basic esports coach training program as well as a specialized CS:GO coach training program. During the basic training program, esport coaches learn to organize and carry out targeted and inspiring training sessions that develop the athletes physically, mentally and socially. Coaches get acquainted with skill-developing exercises and activities and learn how to create positive and inclusive training environments. The basic training program qualifies esports coaches for the more specialized CS:GO B Coach Training Program. During this program, participants get in-depth knowledge of the elements of the game, and acquire tools for effective skill development through mentored practice.

YouSee DGI League
Together with a number of other stakeholders, DGI Esport has formed the official Danish esports league called the YouSee DGI League. The league offers Danish esports teams and clubs an opportunity to compete in a well-organized tournament and to qualify for the regional championships as well as for the official Danish esports championship. The league is for all clubs and teams regardless of their skill level, and attracts teams from all over the country with casual players to seriously competitive players.

Ethics
DGI Esport is acutely aware that the world of esports involves a number of ethical problems and challenges including problems with health, betting, gambling and age restrictions. As a national esports organization, they are obligated to take these problems seriously, and together with a number of other Danish esports related organizations, they have created an Ethical Code of Conduct. The Ethical Code of Conduct deals with issues such as physical and mental health, gambling, drugs and alcohol, gambling, fair play and behavior, and DGI encourages all esports clubs and associations to commit to an ethical code, if not the one presented by them here, Ethical Code of Conduct.

Physical Training
DGI Esport is an enthusiastic advocate of physical training in esports, and helps esports clubs introduce exercise and physical activities to their members. It is a well-known scientific fact that physical activity not only improves the strength of our bodies and our perseverance but also makes our brains work better and boosts our ability to make complex decisions, predict consequences and think ahead.

DGI works to ensure that physical training becomes an integrated part of esports training, because they firmly believe that healthy, strong and fit esports players create the best results. Furthermore, they feel that they have a strong moral obligation towards young esports players, and see it as their duty to educate them on the importance of physical training and the health risks related to a sedentary life style.

Q&A with Martin Fritzen

1. Should grassroots sports organizations enter the esports field? And if so, what approach (including the types of activities) should be used?

Yes, indeed. Esports fit really well with other sports clubs and grassroots sports organizations. What I have learned is that, it is all about relevancy. If you are a grassroots sports club, and you want to include esports, you'll want to ask your local community for their input. Facilitate an informal meeting in the club, invite members of the community, in-and outside of the club, and see if anyone is interested in organized esports activities. Usually they are. From there you will build a project group, which will start to develop and offer relevant esports activities in the club.

The target group should help decide on the types of activities. What do they want? Which games are they interested in? Do they want to become world champs and train eight hours a day? Do they want to play just once a month and have fun with their friends? We see all types of esports activities in Denmark right now. From players sitting at home, to paying members of a club, as well as gamers playing against other online clubs. We see players bringing their own computers to the club for practice and competition. We see clubs renting esports facilities outside of their club; grassroots sports clubs building expensive esports rooms; and clubs spending 60,000+ EUR to build training and competition facilities.

We see big, rich clubs do it. We see small, non-rich clubs do it. Everything works. It all depends on the target group you have in your community and the volunteers you can attract as coaches, project managers and so on.

2. How do you think esports can benefit local sports associations?
Depending on what kind of esports activities you offer we see some different benefits. On the larger scale we see that grassroots sports clubs who are involved in esports get:

• More members
• New target groups as members
• New sponsors
• New volunteers
• New PR/media time
• New activities to offer to markets, parties, festivals etc.

If we consider our social responsibility to our communities, we see that 40% of the esports players have never been members of sports clubs before. When sport clubs start to offer esports activities, they attract new target groups. Some have been lonely. Some are diagnosed with Asperger's or ADHD, some do not have a network, some do not have any friends. This changes when these target groups become members in sports clubs, offering esports. We see these people blossom, gain new friends, new networks – we even see them grow and develop in a positive way in school, because of the positive boost they get from the meaningful esports communities they are part of.

Outro

Whatever you do, focus on quality, it pays off and it attracts more quality.

My name is Martin and allow me to thank you for reading this. I travel the world talking about, teaching, and building grassroots esports clubs plus helping brands to benefit from the movement. Please, do not hesitate to contact me, if I can help you.

The suggestions found in this guide are all based on my personal experiences working to help build grassroots esports around the world. All the advice that I give you has been tried and tested for esports organizations of all sizes, and I hope that it will help yours as well.

Key takeaways in this guide:
1. Develop strong teams and work with great people.
2. Build a unique mission statement based on your core values and vision.
3. Set simple and clear goals.
4. Plan 1, 2, and 3 years ahead.
5. Reduce your costs.
6. Understand why your organization is unique and how you can make a difference to partners
7. Secure the revenue streams you will need to achieve your goals.
8. Understand how you make profit and how you scale your business.
9. Work hard and focus on partnership sales every day.
10. Be quality-oriented in everything you do.
11. Continuous development and learning.

Happy Reading,
Martin Fritzen